Acknowledge

ld like to thank the FBI agent- who is part of the "Charlie's

ls" team, along with my own "Uma Thurman" and her magic

f it was not for your Divine Intervention- I don't believe I

d have lived to see another birthday. Thank you to the Officer

stood in the gap in spite of the oppression, and her career

You are a person of integrity, and I will never forget what you

iced for my son and I. Teri- you are the BEST! Melissa- the

seling I receive from you gives me the tools to conquer many

sters- thank you! Vicki, Mike and my Church! The prayer and

wship you gave the broken woman who showed up Sunday's is

f Jesus Lives! Nita, Jody, Dave, Ginny, T- without you con-

ng to "see" me even when I was invisible- you are the greatest

ples of friendship- YOU ROCK! Also- there are so very many

le who dedicate their lives every day- for meager wages, to

t us- from victims to survivors. Because of what you do- I

not "out" you- however you guys know who you are to me!

Dedication

This book is dedicated to all

Domestic Violence and Sexual Assault Survivors.

I wrote this book to be a supportive road map as you travel your

own dark journey. You're not alone and don't you ever give up!

Explanatory Note

To protect the privacy and identities of key individuals, I have chosen to alter names and locations to otherwise disguise and protect the people involved in my story. Any similarities between fictitious names, places, and real ones, is of course, entirely coincidental.

"Take care how long you battle monsters.
For as you look long into the abyss, the abyss also
looks long into you."
Neitzke

Introduction

This story- my story, really could be anybody's. Domestic violence, sexual assault- isn't a respecter of persons. The monster doesn't play favorites, doesn't prefer blondes, isn't mindful of one's education or financial demographics. It is a random predator, and you cannot tell its prey by where they may shop, or the type of car they drive. She could be a cashier, or he could be a school teacher. I wanted to make sure when you start on this trip down the rabbit hole with me, you think about this. Because if you are a survivor, you must know that nothing you did- now or ever, caused you to deserve the abuse. Nothing! You aren't stupid, it isn't wrong to trust someone, nor is it wrong to love another human being. The wrongness happened when the "person" you trusted began hurting you, and hurting you…and hurting you. Wrongness happens to you when you begin believing under this heaviness, that there is no exit strategy for you. Or when, you no longer have hope for a different life. That is the warped wrongness of the predator's influence and their lie's impact upon your spirit.

Before my life became qualified for a Steven King novel I defined myself as a Mom, a person of faith, a hard worker, an athlete, a good friend with a wacky sense of humor. I had an eclectic group of friends and a positive outlook on life. Once the horror started; it was like being trapped with a suffocating force, held captive in the dark, and forced to watch your life plummet down into an abyss. Your mouth is wide open, but nothing comes out. No exit sign in this dark theatre, and the person you were has vanished, to be replaced by this tightly wound and numb creature- unrecognizable from the self portrait you had of yourself before.

From the Beginning

I was "groomed" for almost 2 years before I said the fateful words, "I Do." Groomed is a term used to describe the controlling and planned behavior of your abuser or predator- to woo or romance their intended victim. Could I tell that I was being "sized up"? Nope. I carried out this dance, cooperatively. I thought this was courtship, and that I was being considered as a partner- by him, the same way I was contemplating him for my future.

Don't you just love hindsight? Looking back, I should have thought more about the way all his friends seemed so aloof, and the lack of community among his small circle of friends. His peer group was mostly composed of men in law enforcement but, none had been in the same agency for very long at a time. I have relatives in law enforcement, and discounted his friends' history of surfing agencies as an economic necessity. He had a large family that gathered together monthly to celebrate birthdays, and had picnics. I believe now, that I was "shopped" for. A "Law Enforcement Barbie" who would be more receptive to his lifestyle choices and advances. He was correct.

By the end of our first year dating, we were living together. He was funny, and charming, and appeared to have the same convictions as myself. I never saw episodes of what I would label anger or rage. Myself, I never had much of what I would call family. I came from a very dysfunctional family- a mother who rivals a black widow spider, and a father who suffered through his own abusive childhood, only to pass it along unbeknownst to him- like a dark gift. I watched for rage, which was a red flag I saw often growing up.

He was not opposed to me being more proficient in some arenas- like horsemanship, which was refreshing to me. I have always been very athletic- shoot, I was the coach for most of the sports my children were involved in. Until now, I kind of had what I called "The Xena Effect" on the men I dated. I show up for an outdoor date, and they see an imagined "S" on the spandex through my under armor. Exit stage right for the 1st timer- running away faster than a competitor in Zombiefest. Here was a man who appeared to enjoy my ability to keep up. He appeared to enjoy my zest for life.

He loves me.

I was a dedicated fiancée. That's the title I earned after helping him put together an executive resume, certifications and credentials that got him a job offer as an executive law enforcement officer out-of-state. What a feeling of accomplishment for me- to know I had contributed in the process of helping my fiancé get his dream position!

The rush was on then- to get everything together for our relocation. First- to be married at home, and then arrive as Mr. and Mrs. VIP.

I should share- I did have a trickle tingle of "spidey sense", which my Dad had taught me. I knew that to hire for an executive position, the city/county/state which employs will do an extensive background check, polygraph, and psychological screen. Daddy didn't raise a stupid girl. When news was returned that my fiancé was hired for the position, I thought everything was substantiated. The tingle must have been moving and wedding jitters, right?

He loves me.

A week following our wedding, I had a first glimpse of The Monster.

I was left behind to organize and do all the packing for the move- while he assumed his new career.

One afternoon I received a screaming call about my moving skills, my intelligence, my laziness, and ineffectiveness- while he was doing "everything" at his new job. The closest way to describe the feeling, is to imagine crossing the street to greet a loved one and having a locomotive magically appear and crush you into the pavement. Kind of like Wile E. Coyote- but you don't get up like he does in the cartoon. I think on it now- it was like having all the breath, all your liveliness, crushed right out of you, and your mouth is wide open, and nothing comes in or out. I think I lasted like that for days. When people asked me how the move was going, I still couldn't find the breath to speak. He called me back 2 days later, like nothing ever happened. Can I say this was the beginning of the "WTF" of my life? This is the phase in the process the professionals call "crazy-making". My life began to travel from one train wreck/ WTF to the next scheduled freight train arrival. Only, this schedule was so random and unpredictable I found myself doing a boxing feint dance, trying to stay on my toes to dodge the next bullet train.

He loves me not.

I heard 1 ½ years into living in shelters as the invisible woman, that

13

one of my dear friends overheard my husband share with one of his law enforcement friends, that "his move would effectively cut me off from my bullshit friends. I'm putting a goddamn stop to it." I wish she had pulled me aside and told me. I would never have left the state to join him. Too often, as women and friends, we don't intervene and disclose a "dark observation". We are afraid it will hurt feelings, or even doubt our own selves and our perception of an evil moment or statement. Please- as brothers and sisters, we must share our concerns for the welfare of each other. We must disclose when we escape from a predator, and warn our friends before they also become a victim! We are the most effective resource we have. Your intuition and observations could save someone in jeopardy.

Well, I bought the, "I am just under incredible stress in starting this new position" line. Surely, no one would really talk to someone doing all the moving that way- really? I had resigned from a terrific job, relocated my son to the new high school, and emptied my own bank account to assist in the moving expenses.

A week before everything was ready for moving, a shadow is discovered on my last minute mammogram with insurance, and I am urgently called in for an ultrasound. I called my new husband for support. Here comes the train! "What the fuck did I expect him to do about it? If I am sick, stay the fuck home!"

He loves me not.

Here's the pitfall I made and dug myself. Sister's- step away

14

from the bullshit and drop your shovel now! When someone we love responds to us in this manner, we work diligently to find "reason" (really an excuse) as to how someone could be so insensitive? I went mentally through my knowledge of his family tree- found members of his family who died of cancer- and stuck my first dip of the shovel in, to start my hole.

It does not take a whole lot of time to dig a hole 6ft deep. Enough to bury your head in- or hide a body. We were not even a month married!

When I arrived at the new location, things were again like when we were dating. Nothing was said about apologizing. Nothing was said about his raging and insensitive behavior, or about my clean bill of health (I forgot to tell you- it wasn't cancer.)

I was "Mrs. Law Enforcement Barbie". I met public officials, subordinates, council members, Chamber of Commerce merchants, and publicity personalities.

He bought me a car for my wedding present. I thought perhaps all the raging was the stress of moving, new job, new wife, and new responsibilities.

I dug another shovelful.

He loves me.

Fade to Blue

As I was traveling across country to our new home, new town, I felt a mixture of excitement and apprehension. I admit, I had hopes that the tension I had felt from my husband would be resolved when everything was finally in place in our new location. As I began to look around at the mountain of boxes and crates, I realized just how physically exhausted I was. After all, my son and I had physically packed all of my husbands 2500 sq ft home, his garage, shop, barn- while he was starting his new position. Would we be getting any help now that we were here? I had this suspicion that everything would once again be piled upon my shoulders for me to unravel in our new home.

Initially- I was invited to accompany him to his various public speaking events, radio interviews, and publicity events. He started out animated about all the changes he was going to bring to this antiquated department.

But, I began to notice (when I could finally see over the stacks of cardboard boxes and newspaper wrapping) that my husband was seldom at home, and when he was- he appeared to be overwhelmed by this promotion sometimes. My invitations to accompany his celebrity became less and less. Like Cinderella, I started getting returned home to get back to scrubbing and unpacking before my carriage became a pumpkin again.

I noticed too, that all the things my husband had said he enjoyed with me while we were dating: hiking, hunting, riding, climbing- all ceased very quietly and gradually.

If he wasn't at work or politicking, he was at the gym.

The "honey doo" projects assigned to me got longer and longer. The lists of things he needed me to accomplish became longer than the hours we had daylight.

I looked up one day and the calendar said I had been married 30 days.

The First Incident

50 days after I arrive to a new place to begin my new life, I see The Tyrant.

My husband arrives home from work, and immediately begins pacing (like a lion in a cage), his voice goes from just shouting to raging. "He hates his job! Everyone is an asshole! The council members are fucking losers! He is quitting this piece of shit job! He is going to quit and move us all out of here" The tirade lasts through dinner and on into the evening. I finally hear in his verbal regurgitation of disgust and anger, how he had met with a local high ranking politician for lunch today. He discovered during their meal, that the politician is running for a second 4 year term, and will then endorse his subordinate for the job. He is raging as he had plans for a quick advancement to greater political power and, now it is dashed. He wouldn't have taken this piece of shit job, knowing that! I am worthless because through my help I put him here! It is my fault! I need to start looking for another job for him immediately!

I find myself slipping in and out of this daisy chain of madness- He loves me, He loves me not. Sometimes he is tender, fun and a kind lover. And then- there are the times he is brutal with his verbal battery and alternating shunning.

56 Days married. I am doing laundry when my husband comes to the laundry room door to exclaim, "I am putting up fence today!" Now. In the wind. And the rain. "Hurry your ass up!! You never help me! Stupid, lazy bitch!" He forcibly recruits my 16 year old son- screaming for him to, "get your shit on and get outside!" This is the first time he has addressed my son in anger- and I am fearful for my son. I ditched the laundry, dressed for the gale force winds and rain outside, and jogged down to the barn. As soon as I arrived, he dismissed my son to go fix himself lunch, and it is creepy quiet while my son drives the truck up to the house. I am alone with The Monster.

My husband asks me to hold up a 12ft railroad tie, so he can backfill the 6ft hole it is sitting in. He is going to push dirt into the hole, operating his excavator. As I stand there, he has a near miss where the bucket of the equipment skips over the ground and almost strikes me, and I jump out of the way. I remember that I gave him a "look". I stared right into his eyes then, long, hard and searching. He then said, "Don't worry, I would never hit you." And he waited a second or two. I moved back into the position he told me to take.

Looking back on the parts I remember- after repeating them to police, sheriffs, and case managers, his voice was "funny". It was flat. It was cold and without emotion.

The next instant, I am struck in the head by the excavator bucket and the railroad tie. I remember flying in the air, and striking the next center post railroad tie, and then darkness. I wake up on the ground facedown in the mud, and could hear a voice inside me just screaming, "GET UP, GET UP, GET UP!!!!!!" and my legs wouldn't work. I was like a bug dying on the ground after being sprayed with Raid. I looked up and saw him, sitting there on the excavator- expressionless. I lost consciousness again, and then woke up to find myself trying to pull myself up on the barbed wire fencing, clutching my face like I'm trying to keep it from falling off. I think I vomited. I then heard my son, screaming from way off, shouting, "What are you doing? Help Her! Help Her Up!!!!"

It wasn't until my son arrived, and I saw his face in the rain, that my husband got off the excavator. He drug me face down, and shoved me into the back seat of the truck. My son (who doesn't have his drivers' license) was told to drive me up to the house. My husband did not come up to the house to check on me for 1 ½ hours.

He love me not.

After midnight, I was still vomiting, my vision wasn't working right, I was so dizzy, and in such pain. I couldn't hear out of my left ear. I couldn't get out of bed, unless I crawled, clutching the carpet. I asked my husband to please take me to the emergency room? He said, "I am fucking watching TV." I crawled down the stairs, and outside. I don't know how I got to the car? It took me 30 minutes to drive the 5 miles to the hospital. The orderly asked me if I thought my husband did it on purpose?

I said I didn't know.

I did tell you that it was a small community we lived in, didn't I? Like Harper Valley PTA, right? After disclosing that little bit to the orderly, I began to feel panic! I had this scared rabbit impulse to get off the table and run out of the building! I thought of how quickly the news of my injury would travel here, and reach back to my husband. What was I going to do? He is a VIP here! Who's really going to believe me? I didn't know anyone here really. He'd made sure of that!

After parading me around in the first two weeks of our arrival in the "Barbie and Ken" sweepstakes, he kept me "busy" doing things for him around our new place. I had a list of expectations to fulfill, which kept me out of public view. I also discovered being the chief's was very restrictive socially. I was not embraced anywhere. I was informed at the local diner, that it would be 8-9 years before "they" would let me in. "The former Honcho's wife was a bitch, and they were not going to let me forget it!"

As I sat there, listening to my heart monitor, I began to hear the echoes of my husband's creepy innuendo's and scenarios. I could then see from my hospital bed in my minds eye, the bottom of that posthole- right where I was struck down.

I recall that one of his favorite scenarios is about burying a wife alive.

As my luck would have it, I got pulled over by a county sheriff as I drove home. I told him I had been in the hospital, and why. He asked why my husband hadn't driven me himself to the hospital after he hurt me? I told him my husband wanted to watch TV.

I guess being the wife of a VIP does have it perks. You can try to kill your wife and not have it truly questioned, and- she doesn't get a ticket when she drives herself home from the hospital afterwards.

I think the "don't talk, don't tell" propaganda, becomes a powerful poison. The longer you stay silent, the easier it is to swallow and the harder it is to ever find your voice. You become brittle, like an old window pane, and the slightest request for the truth causes your whole being to shatter and fragment. I need to tell you- it's ok to be broken when you tell something monstrous is happening to your person, your body, your spirit. Under the disguise of love, you are hurt and your trust and your spirit- everything is broken. The Monster takes your breath. The Monster steals your spirit.

But tell someone! Tell them again! And again!

The Beginning of the Descent

Now I am shunned. Untouched. Unloved. A Leper.

The bank teller knows about the unusual shaped birthmark I have on my bottom because someone in the emergency department leaked my trauma intake. I cannot drive as the vertigo is too severe.

I cannot get outside the house. I cannot job search. My son and I are prisoners.

Yes, when I think I cannot take anymore, his family comes for a surprise visit-joy. The entire visit I am magically transformed back into a beloved wife. We pose merrily for photo opportunities, hugging and kissing. At night, I lay in the dark with The Monster.

Get copies of all your doctors' reports, and keep them in a safe place. I learned from another survivor of OIDV- Officer Involved Domestic Violence- that her abuser used his authority to alter and "disappear" her records. Even when you are able to escape, you may be unable to get back to them- and, you might need them someday. Also- I learned that you may request privacy precautions and protections on your medical files within most hospitals and urgent care facilities. This will prohibit everyone, including a spouse from viewing or gaining access to your information.

I believe I am receiving a stay of execution when my husband asks me quite jovially, to accompany him to a new site for us to rappel. He is planning on opening a teaching gym, and would love my support. My son joins us for the trip into the country. In a quiet moment alone, my husband is speaking with me about a climbing pitch that is quite challenging. I don't have a climbing harness small enough to fit me right now, but he assures me he can make one to fit me- to try this particular climb. He reminds me of what a gifted athlete I am. But…should I veer off the climbing route, the harness he makes for me could pitch me out, and I would fall, probably to my death.

If you are alone in the forest with your husband, and he suggests a way to murder you- if no one else hears him, did it really happen?

I assure him I am not well enough to attempt climbing, as I am still injured from the excavator accident. I now know exactly what a deer in the headlights has going through his head- as he freezes in the highway. My husband leaves without a word for the vehicle. I run and stagger, half frozen inside, to catch my ride home, with The Monster.

You know, I completely disremembered an event of abuse, until taking this long green mile home. It was when he was instructing me on how to belay. My first try, he was in the harness, when he kicked himself off of a hold and off of a rock face. His weight jerks me off my feet, swinging me like a human hammer, into the rock face. Somehow, I brought both feet up into my chest as I slam into the wall, now feet first. My knees drive into my chest, and I am jerked back and forth into the wall again and again as he runs along the rock face, laughing hysterically.

After we were married, he is belaying me on a rock face that is about 85 feet up- a 5.9 in difficulty. As I perform a dynamic move to cross a crevasse to reach for a niche in the rock, he pulled me from the 50 foot rock ledge, and I swing like a pendulum to crash into the apposing rock face. I kicked off, and as I am dropped, my arms flailing, I caught a small ledge with my arms, and hung there. People were looking up at me, and I could hear my husband then-making excuses for how I fell. He is exclaiming to the shocked people below that I was, "trying something too tough for my skill level" and getting in a bind. I pulled myself up on the ledge, unsnapped myself from his belay, and sit on the ledge, shaking like I have hypothermia in the 80 degree heat. I free climb to the ground, but I cannot get into the car with him. Why/how could someone who loves me do a stunt like this? This was before the excavator incident. I never climb with him again.

I have begun to journal everything that has happened to me. So far, he has only yelled at my son once, but I decide, never again! I will have to double my efforts to gain employment, so my son and I can escape! How do I do that when I still am suffering vertigo from the excavator incident?

I am so afraid my husband will find my journal, that I bury it out in the woods where I walk with my dogs. I will keep track of everything that happens so if I disappear, I will leave someone the message where to find it- and so they can take my son away from here. I have to think of someone whom I can trust to tell everything to, but who?

I copy my journal entries when my husband is away- and begin forwarding it to several friends back in my hometown.

I don't discuss the specifics of my abuse, but my son and I

decide we are going to leave as soon as I get an income of my own. He will never be alone with his step-father, ever. I make our exit strategy- who to tell, where to run, whom to call, what numbers- and my son and I review them like prisoners of war.

I know how in the middle of Armageddon, how can you think to journal? Do!! I was advised that rape victims, victims of trauma and violence don't remember everything after their assaults. That memory comes back like Swiss cheese- with holes in it, that is remembered more over time. I think we are less like cheese and more like trying to put together a target after it has been blasted by a shotgun. Little pieces scattered like confetti on the ground- and it takes time to see if the target can be put back together like it was before the blast.

Keeping a journal also keeps your memory honest. Brutally honest. Someday, you will be shocked at what your mind dropped, to keep you sane. You can bury the parts of the assault your body and mind cannot carry while trying to survive, in your journal- where it can be used for evidence later.

My son and I join a church in town. We left all our friends and church community to come here, and I figured we should try to assume some kind of normal life. Although there are quite a few different agency officers and their families as members, we try to blend in. We volunteer for anything that will get us out of the house, and create some kind of new friend base. We begin hearing back small fragments of the propaganda that has been sabotaging my son and I in meeting new people, and gaining a job. I am being told that folks were surprised to discover that my son and I really do like their small town after all! It seems that my husband had been telling business people and shop owners that both my son and I hated it here, and wished to leave. This must be why I get no calls back from any of my applications. I join a bible study, and finally find a small piece of peace in the middle of this tornado to beat anything Dorothy ever faced! I have always been a person of faith, and it is comforting to be within a church again.

My son and I begin asking for prayer- just random prayer, after each worship service. Since everyone knows about the excavator incident, I do ask for healing from the "accident". We cannot risk being specific about anything else, but have to believe that God knows why we are here. People think I have tears because the bible word that Sunday is touching, but I am crying because we really, really need God to rescue my son and I! I notice that my husband appears jealous, that I have been able to pick up my faith and pursue it here. Although he tries to orchestrate jobs and last minute trips now for us to be away from our church and community, for the first time, I resist.

My son and I became friends with a woman whose husband is a retired chief of police. I think my husband is afraid I will tell her something if he keeps trying to create drama about my faith, so he stops badgering me about our time at church.

We both begin to have some social activities from our church membership, and my son and I felt a little lighter in our hearts and footsteps.

I receive a job offer to be a school resource officer, and to do some limited law enforcement for another town. At first, my husband seems proud that his Barbie gets a uniform. My husband with all his expert skills, is entrusted by my new law enforcement boss, to train me in the areas of self-defense and weapons handling, to keep me safe.

My husband tells me he is not going to train me, even while he lies to the other chief. He also takes back my service revolver for my new job. I resign before I begin. I cannot tell the other chief, why I won't be safe to perform the duties. It will get back to my husband, and there will be hell to pay.

I am alone at home and am surprised when my husband grabs my arm- it seems it is time to put up fence again. He escorts me down to the bottom of the property, where you cannot be seen from the house or the road. I am afraid, so afraid, that I won't be coming back up the hill again. This time, he forces me to drive the excavator, like he is daring me to hit him and then we will be even? I don't want to drive it!

I never have driven an excavator! I stand there and don't move, while he commands me louder and louder, to get on! Again and again, he tells me to drive a fencepost into the ground, move the bucket, while he stands under it. I am soaking wet through my clothing 30 minutes later and shaking. I just jump off, and start running up to the house, but stop and throw up. I shout over my shoulder while I run to the house, that I will never drive the excavator again.

One of the things every predator does, before pulling down its prey for the kill- is isolate it from its "pack" or "herd". We were smart to continue to press out and about within the community, no matter how we felt, as I was still suffering from my assault injuries. We unknowingly became a more difficult target for him- mingling amongst our "herd". It was vitally important to keep in church. We so desperately needed to keep faith, to hope, when someone so powerfully opposed was trying to take it away.

Don't Close Your Eyes

Even now, I don't know how to start talking about it. I get this big lump in my throat, and my chest feels like an elephant is standing on it. My eyes get wet in the corners, and- I am sitting here at the computer, feeling a slow growing numbness like how ocean fog rolls onto the boardwalk, and slips through a town in a horror film.

My husband had not attempted to be intimate with me, since the assault with the heavy equipment. He would deliberately stay up after I went to bed, with the TV turned up really loud, until he thought I was asleep. After his family left, he made a comment that he was only putting on a show while his family was here, and not to get used to it. He off-handedly says he finds me disgusting, and isn't sexually interested in me any longer.

I was sound asleep when all of a sudden the covers were snatched off of me and he is on top of me. He grabs my ankles, and pulls my legs apart, without ever making a sound. This assault is so quick I have hardly even realized it's my husband, and I am rigid with fear and frozen in place. My groin muscles strain and scream as they are wrenched apart while I resist. I don't think I want to tell you the graphic details. I still feel ashamed when I tell it. He bites my inner thighs, my pelvic floor, my most delicate female parts- he's so aggressive that I am bleeding. Still he is silent, like an assassin. I am completely paralyzed, and holding my breath, shaking my head slightly like I will wake up and discover that I am not really being raped. I have a hand over my own mouth, so I won't scream and wake my son. He then grabs my hair, and drags me around, and shoves my face into his groin. I do what he is silently demanding for. He gets up, goes into the bathroom, and I still cannot believe what has happened to me.

I reach between my thighs, and come away with blood on my hands. He comes back to bed, still silent, rolls over and goes to sleep. I am afraid to get up and see where the blood is coming from. I don't want to see what happened to me. I lie on my side, right on the edge of the bed, and cry as quietly as I can. I don't want to wake The Monster.

Daybreak. He kisses me and says, "Good Morning" and adds

that, "Every woman needs to be fucked." He goes into the bathroom and starts his shower. I put on my robe, and stiffly walk downstairs to where his service revolver is in its holster. And, I look at it.

As I walk back upstairs with the feeling of dried blood on my body, I stand outside the bathroom door and picture in my mind what it would be like to empty his own service gun into the shower stall-into The Monster. The glass will explode, and I would fire until I hear the gun click and click and click- that it has no more bullets. I have to empty the gun, because I can't be sure he won't get up again- he is like a monster in a horror movie. They too-keep coming and coming, and no one stops them! His blood will be caught in the shower, and pass down the drain. But I also tell myself, that no one would believe that such a man of importance abuses his wife, rapes his wife and, I would go to jail and my son would be alone. I would never see my son again. So I put on my clothes, over the blood, and head downstairs like a good wife to make breakfast for my husband.

Later my husband keeps bragging over and over, about "ravishing" me, now saying that he loves me. By attacking me, now everything is normal between us? I still have not left the place where I was a worthless human being. It takes me over a week to get the courage to look back at that night, and to add rape to my hidden journal. Within the next 10 days he gives away my car, his wedding present to me.

I think somewhere within this timeframe, I remember it was after the rape, I made a dynamic decision, to decide what parts of me I was going to make the serious intent to hold on to. To resist, while the control and domination of my husband ultimately tries to destroy every part that makes me unique, that makes me, me. I was being whittled down with surgical skill, and I thought there might be a time when I didn't know myself anymore. I decided then that my son, my freckles, and my faith, were the things I would stand up for. I didn't think I could make a stand about any-thing else. I remember making this small list of the things I love, to hide in my journal and keep safe.

First, were my children, friends, and family- but there were other things too. I sat in the woods while he was at work and my son at a friend's home, and felt like I was having to emergency evacuate my life onto several lines in my journal, and then face a natural disaster like hurricane survivors or tornado victims do. I began packing memories of camping trips and swimming with my children, the smell of fresh cut hay, and puppies breath, Black eyed Susan's & daisies, the smell under a horses mane and the feel of a fast horse underneath you. I cried as I put my journal into the plastic bag and buried it again.

Years after the rape, when I finally have the courage to be intimate, I had significant bleeding again, due to the damage done to me by my husband. Marilyn Monroe has a quote I have felt a connection with. She said, "I have never been bitten by a dog. Only by humans."

I am still suffering from the ringing in my ears and the huge headaches. While lying in bed one evening, I hear the TV, and it is "Silence of the Lambs". I get up to really see if that is what is on, as my husband had said during our dating that he hates horror movies. I look over the railing, and my husband begins imitating Hannibal's speech, about the lambs. He begins telling me how in his expertise of criminology, he would have done it differently, and- he would have gotten away with it.

I feel sick to my stomach while he is talking about cannibalism. His hand is down his pants, and he is touching himself. His voice sounds like it did when he was talking to me from the excavator. The dark echo of his reptilian tone keeps me awake all through the night.

I must get better for my son and I to escape! I decide to make an appointment with a doctor out of town to avoid any possible rumor. It is here, with the nurse, that I finally let the poison out.

I tell her about my husband assaulting me, his attempts and threats of murder and verbal abuse, that my son and I are being kept like prisoners, and the details of the rape. I beg them not to say anything outside the office, because I think he will kill me rather than ruin his reputation. I get a ride to the physician out of town with the excuse it's my woman annual, but really, ist because I have these blinding migraines, vertigo, and I still cannot hear. The diagnosis isn't helpful- bones are broken inside my skull, bones for hearing. I may never get my hearing back. I may have vertigo for the rest of my life, along with the headaches.

A Little Light

On his orders to bring 'his shit' from home to the office, I go to my husband's office. I see one of the officers who works for him. She tells me he is not in. He told her to advise me that he, "couldn't wait around for me". Ann comments that she heard about the "accident".

She describes how it seems my husband gets "seen" regularly clutching his face in his hands, murmuring regretfully, "I almost killed my wife" - for all the other officials and officers to see. She is staring at me intently, and I start to cry. "Are you alright?" "No, I am not." And, then a little miracle happens as she begins to speak. Ann discloses to me that she has thought my husband was a son of a bitch since she first shook hands with him his first day on the job! And, she shared this with the other officers too. Ann said he is just like the monster she used to work for, in another place and time. She said she didn't believe any of my husband's bullshit, and that she thought his stories of valor didn't match up to what his resume said. Did I think he lied on his federal application, because the stories didn't match? Then Ann asks me, "He did it on purpose, didn't he- the assault?"

I tell my new friend Ann, my ally, every single thing that has happened. We leave the city, so no one sees us together. She shares his bullying of others with me; officers, the dispatchers, wives of officials and of missing weapons unaccounted for.

Then- like an avalanche, Ann shares that the city never did a background check, polygraph, or a psychological screening on my husband! I am totally blown apart by her statement! They were dazzled by his resume and his interview, and didn't want to spend the money.

Oh my God! My spidey sense was tingling for a very good reason! I am not stupid, and not the only one fooled either. Ann gives me her personal number and email, for me to forward my journal entries- and, I begin copying her as well.

I cannot use our home computer, as I am unsure if he has the ability to check out what I write, or where I search. I have to be very careful when I go to the local library as it is right next to the cop shop- and he watches and notes whenever my son and I are there. I tentatively sit down at the computer in the library and Google search the man who is my husband. I discover protection orders (which should have prohibited him from even being a security guard), and multiple domestic violence reports. The resume he had me write for him, doesn't match his credentials or certifications.

I discover a woman named on a lawsuit as his wife- that no one ever mentioned or knows about. And, she is missing.

I dig deeper. I find newspaper articles of a failed political campaign of his. Failed as he was caught in fraud and misrepresentations, and let go from his duties. Ann and I swap information and we are both greatly frightened for my son and I.

We have been receiving hang up calls since 2 weeks after we move into our new home. My husband says it happens all the time with land lines, as they used to belong to someone else. But, the calls begin to have heavy breathing, and seem to only happen when He is at work? Then, I am not getting any of our household bills on line anymore. I call the phone company and discover that our phone privacy codes have been hacked, and all our information has been forwarded to a different email address. A pornographic address? Immediately after putting a stop to the billing transfer, my email address is hacked, my name is stolen, and I begin receiving pornographic messages and photos of my husband with another woman, and multiple women, and this woman with a dog. My children at college get the photos, as she has accessed my address book, and is stalking my children. It seems my husband is a star of some intense internet pornography. I tell my husband about the theft, and he is very bland about it. I press the issue about the porn, and the photos, and that I am going to report it, and he gets really angry!

He then reveals he is being blackmailed by this woman, and has been for quite sometime. I cannot tell, as then she will send it to the local news. We are forbidden to report it but my son and I have a reprieve of peace, while my husband battles the woman from his past.

Thank goodness my Nancy Drew-ness is alive and well. I copied all the internet news articles, court proceedings, protection orders, credentials and his federal application. I sent them to Ann, and hid hard copies of it too. Later, I would have it all, along with my journal to forward as a part of the investigation. Amidst all the intimidation and crazy making that was done to me- during my abuse, I always had my journal and evidence to keep me sane and on track during questioning.

The Shadow Comes

My son and I are all alone, baling the hay on our property. Of course- when you have a woman and child to do your heavy labor for you, why bother to assist? We have the radio on really loud, so we can sing along while we throw hay. Gosh, it is one of the few times we get to listen to our music, as when he is home- it is only what he likes. Suddenly, without any clue why, my son pops a huge nosebleed. We try and try but cannot get it to stop. While we wait, my son begins telling me how he is feeling tired all the time and cannot seem to ever get enough sleep. He thinks he is losing weight although he is eating just the same as always. Then, he asks me to check out this bump/lump he has in his armpit- and I do. After my brush with the mammogram and the threat of "C", I am instantly on alert. We quit for the day, because I ask him to go into the bathroom and shower, but while he is in there- to check out his body for other bumps. I show him how his lymph system runs and where to search. I am waiting outside the bathroom door, as he does a self-examination. He comes out of the shower with his towel on, and we both discover he has lumps like grapes in a vineyard- under his arms, and he tell me the same kind of lumps are in his groin area. It seems the timing of finding them is Providential- the cancer Relay for Life is in 2 days, and I will ask everyone who is the best doctor to take my son to see?

It is also weird as my husband is the "Master of Ceremonies" of the event. I do disclose at the event to the "Master of Ceremonies" that my son needs to see a specialist right away. I was hoping for a little compassion to be thrown my son's way, but we were told to drive ourselves to the event, as the "Master" needed to greet his fans. I do find out, that the doctor to whom I had disclosed the domestic violence is also one of the local specialists for cancer within our area. (I think God was watching.) This begins a shadow time for my son and I. My son has 2 biopsies, and is placed on several different medications, and I watch him lose more weight, and he becomes a little grayer each day.

Non- Hodgkin's Lymphoma becomes a Google search for both of us, as we try to learn about the disease they are hoping to rule out. Weeks go by, and then months and he is not getting better. He has lost 30 lbs, and he sleeps all the time.

When it rains it pours, right? Well, we get an extra early snowstorm, and now my son and I are snowed in. My husband has a city vehicle that can make the ¼ mile long driveway trip to the road, but my son and I are snowbound. We spend several days hoping that we will get a melt and be able to get out of the house but, it snows again and again.

We do have a tractor (or I should say, my husband does) but it doesn't run. We are fast approaching another appointment for my son to see the specialist and we will have to cancel due to the storms. My son is a whiz mechanic, and with a day long dedication to the dozer- he gets it up and running and plows the driveway so we can finally get out. That evening at dinner, instead of a "thank you", my husband begins to raise his voice about something at work, and then changes his focus towards my son, who is trying to finish his dinner. He begins to curse my son, and belittle his efforts at fixing the tractor, and then to scream at him, for plowing the driveway without his express permission! My son gets smaller and smaller, and as I stand there, I see my son clutch his silverware, as my husband rises and starts to step into my son. As my husband begins to lean over my son, I step between them, and I take his wrath and attention, drawing his focus like a bullfighter waving

44

the cape. My son dumps his plate into the sink, and runs to his bedroom. I receive the brunt of my husbands' anger and disgust, but my son gets away.

Without a sparring partner, my husband seems to run out of steam, and leaves to go back to the office, thank God. I go to see how my son is, and we begin to cry together. My son says he is ashamed at himself, as he thought about stabbing my husband if he tried to hurt him tonight.

He thought, as did I, that he was close to laying his hands on my son in anger. I told my son I would never let that happen! We make a pact together, my son and I. We will both try to never be alone with him. And, if my son hears me screaming, he will not come to my rescue- ever. He will run outside, lock himself in the truck, and dial 911 while he drives away. He will be safe. Don't come for me! Call Officer Ann and go to her home. Don't look back! I cannot bear to think about the possibility of my husband hurting my son.

The Monster may get me before I know what is wrong with my sons' health, and get it fixed. My son and I will be here only long enough to have the insurance pay for a great doctor. But, The Monster will never get my son!

The Rabbit finds Her Voice

Several nights later, my husband is amorous. We are in bed, and he is interested in sex, but he begins talking about himself, and his feelings about suicide? This is a strange topic for foreplay. I am quiet as he explains that he thinks a man who commits suicide is a pussy. He says he would kill the problem, not himself. He asks me then- if I would ever commit suicide?

I am only half listening to him, because I still cannot get the image of him raging at my son at the dinner table out of my mind. And, suddenly I know exactly what I am going to say. *(I lower my voice and begin speaking suggestively, as I kiss him and fondle him).* I share that I would never commit suicide. I feel the same way as he does. I see myself as a lioness does, about my young. If anyone hurt my children *(as I climb on top of him. I nibble on his neck and ears as I whisper)* I would do nothing. Until, one night while he is sleeping *(as I am lowering myself on top of him- and he is very excited and thinking of what I will do for him sexually)* I will *(and I stick my fingers like a gun under his throat and jaw line)* blow his fucking head off all over the headboard. I will wipe the gun off on his body- get dressed and call the police and meet them at the door.

It will be worth the "three hots and a cot" to never have my children touched again. *(All this I say to him in a suggestive whisper.)* He is speechless and frozen in place. I get off of him, roll on my side, and look him in the eyes. He gets out of bed, muttering about me being crazy and goes into the bathroom. We never complete the sex act. He never says a word. He removes all his guns from the house while my son and I are at his doctors' appointment. He never ever again acknowledges my son, asks for any favors, or help, he never gives him a ride, or ever asks him to do his grunt work.

I mean it. He may hurt me. He may kill me before I can escape. But if he ever touches my children, I don't care what they will do to me…one morning he won't wake up.

The Downhill Slide

We also begin getting threatening calls from creditors. Apparently my husband is delinquent on his bills. We have always had separate accounts and finances until we moved here. I never knew that almost all of his belongings are leased or on a loan. I begin to compile a list of what he owes- and it is staggering. The total- including his former home is almost $750,000. If they had done a background check he could never have hidden this under a rug. He begins to pressure me about doing his follow through on contacting his creditors, but they won't let me speak to them. My name isn't on those bills thank goodness, and they insist on speaking only with him.

Their pressure begins slowly, to call him at his office during work hours. He calls me to come in to see him, and then begins screaming about the calls, that it is my fault they are calling him because I refuse to help him! He grabs my arm and pushes me down the police department hallway, and shoves me backwards out the door!

My husband begins writing threatening emails to me, demanding for me to intercede with his creditors, or else.

I stop accessing my email, as between the porn from his old girlfriend, and the nasty grams I receive from him at his office, I can't keep up. Over the next several months- the creditor calls escalate right alongside the verbal abuse I receive from my husband. He has several repossessions occur; his truck, his Mercedes, his horse trailer.

His former home is foreclosed upon. I also get a threatening email from The Monster's pornographic co-star. She is threatening to come to town to meet me for the city's July 4th celebration. Can't wait...

My son is required to have a second biopsy sent to a pediatric cancer specialist, and we are scared! I am soon to be graced with a pop-in holiday visit from his psycho porn queen, still suffering post concussion symptoms, without a vehicle (after my wedding present was given away) and the repossession of all the vehicles. Ah, and my husband moves a new officer recruit into our home. To be honest, I don't know if a person can survive holding their breath, but I think I was doing that all the time.

My Barbie smile begins to melt like wax. Ann calls to check in on me as I am not getting out again, within any transportation.

I break down and tell her about the rape, the pornography, the creditors, and the potential guest star for the July 4th parade. Ann tells me then, that she could not stand by and watch him hurt us anymore. She had copied my journal and tried to give a copy to the city prosecuting attorney (in charge of hiring city employees). She also shared about my husbands fraud on his federal application, and that there are guns missing from the police inventory. The city prosecuting attorney refuses to receive it, to even touch her copy, and she left a copy on his desk. She also took a copy of it to the county sheriff's office. She even had it stamped. This was a month ago! She thought surely someone would have contacted me, or questioned me or offered to help! Oh my God!

Are we going to get out of here alive?

My son and I ask the pastor of our church, if there could be a call for prayer as my son's 2nd biopsy has been sent to specialists. The whole church gets up, and together the entire congregation stretches out their hands and prays that my son will receive a good report, it will not be cancer, and our physician will have an answer for his sickness. One of my friends asks me after the service, if I need prayer?

Another woman enters our circle of secrets. She begins to become more active in helping us get out of our home, and have reasons for being about within the community.

One week later, I receive an excited call from my sons' nurse confirming that it is NOT cancer, and that the doctor believes he has the right medication to get him well again! Both of us were crying together! Thank you Jesus! We did the "snoopy dance" around the kitchen and had ice cream! Our celebration was short, as we must behave when The Monster gets home. I made sure I wrote this good news in my journal.

I begin searching for answers to "how could this be happening to us? What can we do?"

I discover several websites: behindthebluewall.com, abuseofpow-er.org and OIDV.org. All about officer involved domestic violence. The facts are staggering. Through these sites, I received a vacuous acknowl-edgement that I am not the only one. The illustration of the abuse cycle wheel is there, and what a difference in that cycle when the abuser is in law enforcement. Did you know that statistics have something like 49% of OIDV victims not living through their escape plans? There is also a national website for all the shelters in the US and their services. I anonymously contact an out of town DV shelter and discover that most shelters do not accept boys over 12 when their mother is running. I will not go without my son! Did you know that most shelters do not have any place for your beloved pets? I was told to get a home for mine before I ran. I placed my horse just before running, but would not leave until I found a place that would take my son and our dog! Did you know that statistics overwhelming show how many domestic violence victims don't leave because their abuser is using their pets as hostages. It is a common and scary threat made by abusers to injury/main or kill the family's beloved pets unless the victim complies. The statistics are staggering also, about how many abusers begin injuring family pets just before they become physically violent with the family. He shot one of my dogs about 30 days before we ran.

My son gets a vehicle. We now have a way to get out of the house, without using his vehicle. The city mechanic questions my son, as it appears he heard from my husband that my son's truck is for sale, and he was going to give the money to my husband for it? We tell him it doesn't belong to the "Great and Powerful Aahz" and it is not for sale.

I also find out that the city mechanic was instructed by my husband to forget looking for a vehicle for me. No wonder I wasn't hearing anything back. My husband has another vehicle of his and a horse trailer repossessed right from our driveway. I find it curious that no one from the city building wondered why a repo-man was asking for directions to the chief of police's home. Did you know that getting vehicles repossessed is cause for termination when you are in law enforcement? I did.

Speaking of vehicles- my wedding present (you remember, the one he took back) has been involved in an accident, and has several tickets attached to it, that are trying to find a way back to me. Why? Because "Genius" never transferred the vehicle title into the other persons name. What a great way to ground me, by messing with my DMV record.

Things get…weird-er. My husband begins exposing himself to me at home. Through the windows, down the stairs, outside when I am working horses. He starts not wearing underwear, and exposing himself while he is watching TV.

The Plot Thickens

My husband wakes me up abruptly, to tell me he is thinking about applying for an executive position in another state. He begins telling me his "game plan". He is going to "push Ann" harder, as she is the only officer he has with seniority to take over when he is gone. He is certain he can train her to run the town as he would- after he moves. Then, he drops the bomb...He will need to make me the "fall guy", and tell everyone how much I fucking hate living here! He will tell everyone how I hate the people, the job opportunities, (shit! Didn't I tell you he had been sabotaging me already? I guess this makes it legit if he can bully me into agreeing?) and that I was making him move! He actually repeated it back another time, this great plan of his. I guess the look I had on my face made it bear repeating? Ah yes, he said, "if I make you the bad guy and I don't get hired, the mayor and the city council will still support me. Don't you see what I am saying", he asks? "Oh yes", I said. "I see exactly where you are going with this. If they do not hire you anywhere else, everyone here will hate me; I will be the bad guy to everyone here. I will not have a friend, or a way to get a job here anymore."

He got up and stormed out of the house, yelling that he'd have to think of another way and slammed the door! I didn't know if I had been holding my breath while I spoke the truth or not, and it hurt to unclench my fists.

I get a phone call from the police station, he is demanding I show up immediately to explain how I had compiled his transcripts for his all and out job quest. He doesn't have any college education, and wishes me to do some "magic" and get his trainings certified to look better. My son and I are in town already, and we head over to the PD. While we are in his office, he is displaying guns that have been donated to the PD or have been confiscated. He calls us back into his office as we are leaving, saying he has something to show my son, when he points and pulls the trigger on a tazer he is pointing at my son!

We both jump around the corner, hearing the snapping sound and I caught a glimpse of the electricity passing across the poles of the tazer. He is laughing like a crazy man, as my son and I pick ourselves off the floor! He is laughing so hard it is difficult to understand, as he explains he didn't have the darts in yet and begins to load the tazer. We both run from the police department, and I report it to the city officer.

Did you know officers are terminated for displaying recklessness with their weapons? Even playing around? Nothing was ever done. Still- there is no contact about the abuse, no case number, nothing.

He overdraws our checking account and I discover his bags are packed. Apparently, he did not get a call back about the first out of state position, but he is driving there anyway to "dazzle them". Now to add to the 178,000 dollars in debt, our checking account is overdrawn by $2300. He shares after dinner, that he admires sociopaths and gives me a list of their admired qualities. It is a portrait of himself. He adds that sociopaths are whatever they need to be, so they can blend in and use their environments.

Like Hanibal Lecter.

My son and I have no money and bare necessities as he leaves to wine and dine the other department heads.

The "conquering whatever" comes home 2 weeks later, and yells at me into the night. I guess I am the cause of ALL his problems! He moves my side of the bed over to where it is up against the sliding glass doors in our bedroom. The cold comes right through onto me, and it is winter. I get an electric blanket and begin wearing several layers of clothes to bed- to keep warm. I am called a frigid bitch because I won't sleep naked next to him and freeze in the drafts from the window.

He begins hoarding his paycheck, and the only bill being paid is our rent. I guess you cannot be a jailer and keep prisoners without a holding cell, right?

He does receive a call back from his wine and dine department, lies to the city about being ill, and leaves again.

I get a call from Ann, to meet her in a café outside of town. She asks me right away, if my son and I had plans to be out of state for Christmas? Shoot, we don't have enough money for groceries, let alone a trip! How are we supposed to go? He gave away my vehicle? She then shares that my husband was passing it around among the police department that my son and I were not happy here, and were going to take an extended trip out of the state to visit family. Ann feels that he has made plans to harm both my son and I, and that our bodies would never be looked for as everyone would just believe we left town.

Maybe another attempt at planting me in the pasture?

I call my husband on his trip, but he doesn't answer. I leave a message for him. Something about receiving several goodbyes from officers who thought I was going out of the state for the holidays, while he was away-hmm? I assured him I had told everyone, even the mayor- that my son and I were spending the holidays at home.

Gee, on an officers wages we couldn't afford to take a vacation, much less leave my beloved husband at home. He never responded to my sugary message; however I am sure he got it.

He returns and we discover he has bought a pickup truck for himself, and gotten nothing for anyone else for Christmas. Happy Holidaze!

Public Displays of Affliction

Three days after Christmas, my son and I are in the local diner, eating lunch. My son has gotten a job at a local store, and we are celebrating his good fortune. My husband comes into the restaurant, in uniform, grabs my arm and pulls me outside the diner. He begins screaming at me for leaving his lights on in his new truck. (I was allowed to drive the truck, to go grocery shopping, and do his errands.)

He grabs my arm, and shoves me back into the cab, still screaming. I look up over the seat, and see a diner full of faces, watching him go off on me. He still has me by the arm, as I try to head back into the diner. We are standing in front of the big picture window of the diner, when I finally tell him, "Let me go! You have no right to treat me like a dog here. In the name of Jesus get back into your police car and get the hell out of here. You have no right to do this in front of folks who are my friends." Oooh he is very angry at me! He finally looks up and there are all those faces, looking right back at him.

I hear back the next morning through Ann, that there were 3 detectives sitting in the diner, and they saw everything! Apparently they had a sheriff's department meeting, and decided that my husband was escalating, becoming more dangerous, to be displaying that kind of anger in public and in uniform! They advise me through Ann, that my son and I need to get out of the house! They make a departmental decision to treat a 911 call from our home very seriously. Ann takes this information to the city's internal affairs department, and they do nothing.

No- wait, they did do something. They have The monster sign a waver for his omissions from his law enforcement application- you know, where he lied about ever having an arrest record. And then, they give my husband a permanent contract to be their police chief.

My husband now is saying I am defective, damaged sexually because I have friends who are gay or lesbian: it's because they haven't been targeted yet by him as a threat. He continues to belittle all my friends until no one will come over anymore. Between scapegoating me for his failed political aspirations and harassing anyone who would befriend me, It is very hard to find any light in this darkness.

One of his few times helping to feed the horses, he becomes angry at me, and strikes me with a 115# bale of hay, knocking me to the ground. He tells me to unload the rest by myself, and drives away, spitting gravel in my face, hair and body.

Ann both encourages and even gets angry with me, to try to make me talk to the local domestic violence representative from the YWCA.

But, I am afraid to talk to her. Ann pressures, cajoles, even begs me to please tell her everything, but The Monster told me he could sleep with the YWCA woman anytime he wants, as she is "hot" for him. Finally, I meet with her, and I discover after finally meeting with her, that not only is she not interested in him, she sees through his façade. I ask her to promise she will not forward any of the information I give her. Without any assistance from either the city or county law enforcement or council, I am afraid he will complete his promise to kill me and my son and I will not get away. I receive some good information and referrals from the YWCA, and pursue them.

At this time I find out there are a lot of women's shelter that will not take boy children of certain ages. We did not have a shelter that would help us, as my son was now 17 yrs old. In our desperation we just thought for sure, as a family we would all have a place within a domestic violence shelter. Please be advised if you have boy children approaching the age of accountability. Our escape was severely postponed as I wouldn't go without him and we hadn't known to look for other alternatives. During this time the YWCA encouraged me to report to the state police. Although I made a full report, nothing was done. I continued to get the line "conflict of interest", because everyone knows The Monster.

July 4th Fireworks

4th of July and I had been told by The Monster that I needed to "ride along", to see what exactly a law enforcement executive does for a living. I witness a traffic stop he makes with a minor, in which he immediately begins verbally assaulting a teen. I sit in the car with a front row seat through his squad car windshield. As I watch, I know if the teen files a complaint I will be asked to make a statement, what am I going to do then? I also know my husband left his police car video camera back at the station, even though the mayor ordered them all to carry their cams. He used words like "little fat fuck" trying to anger and taunt the youth. At one point the kid said he wanted to kick my husbands ass, and my husband goaded him with, "I'd like to see you try!"

I reported it in secret to both the city and county police and found out that my husbands officers had witnessed 3 other incidents where he had badgered and roughed up youths. One officer told the mayor. The rest remained silent. Nothing was done.

I am taken back to the "cop shop" where I listen to my husband crack jokes about the level of domestic violence tolerated in our town to a group of city and county officers. It seems in two decades there have been many arrests, but no one is ever taken to court. My husband comments to the laughing men, "It seems you can beat the fuck out of your wife here, and get away with it."

Does someone become a bit of a monster, if they do not stop one, once he reveals himself? If so- there were a lot of monsters in that parking lot that evening.

The Vacation to Hell

I am recruited by my husband to take a trip across the country. It seems he has requisitioned several autos from the military to place into our police department motor pool, as well as connected himself with another possible executive position, and he needs me to drive one of the vehicles home. I was placed upon the city insurance to be able to drive the chief's auto, but also to drive the "new" police vehicles home.

The trip starts out like we are on a honeymoon. He is excited about meeting the officials from the next potential department, and is singing and doing his impressions of country western singers and voiceovers while we make the 2500 mile trip. He asks what I want for dinner, and actually is kind to me at bedtime. He says he is sorry for the way the job stress has made him act, and I am waiting like the heroine in a Hitchcock film, for the monster to come out.

We arrive at our destination, and as the south should be in the summer, it is hot, humid, and blistering. My husband begins to curse the weather, and then begins to rage. He discovers that the vehicles are not what he thought they would be, and have mechanical problems that will require repairs before we can transport them home. He begins charging costs to the city they never were informed about, and in the middle of my husbands charging spree, they cut off funds and we are stranded without any money, and no room. Can you guess how hot things really got then? Remember, he has overdrawn our checking account so we don't have any money of our own to bail us out?

Amidst the calls to the city to approve more funds, his raging at me is like hands around my throat, just squeezing the life out of me. I am terrified!

We are like a zillion miles away from home, and what is he going to do to me, now that things have gone sideways?

We are now going to tow one of the vehicles home, but I cannot get used to the trailer brakes, they are grabbing on one side whenever I stop- skidding behind the tow vehicle. We are in the parking lot of a big shopping center and he begins to scream at me, of what a "Stupid Worthless C--- I am!!! Get out of the car!! You cannot be taught anything!!!! Find your own fucking way home!!" He grabs for me but I stop the car, grab the car keys, my one bag, and begin running across the parking lot.

66

He continues to rage out the window about how worthless I am, while I shout over my shoulder, "You can have the keys back to the PD vehicle, only after you give me money for a greyhound back home. I have no money and I will not be left here without a way home!" I begin jogging to a fast food restaurant across the parking lot. When I get inside, I am crying, and ask the staff to call 911 if the man in the car outside who has been yelling at me comes inside here and touches me or tries to take my car keys. He comes inside the restaurant, and orders me to come outside with him. I refuse. I told him I would not move until he gives me money for a greyhound bus. I wait 30 minutes, and he drives off with the one vehicle. I ask the employees to watch out for me, and I head over to the pay phones on the bank wall across the street.

I call Ann, and tell her what is happening. I ask her to get my son out of town if I never come back. To tell my son I love him, and for Ann to report me missing to the state police, if I don't get home.

My husband comes up behind me in his vehicle, and gets out, pulling on his hair and red-faced. He says to me, "I am sorry. Please get back into the car. I will drive the one pulling the trailer." I stand there frozen in 100+ degree heat. At least I have made a way for my son to escape if I don't get home alive.

I have no way to get home, and I don't know if I will ever see my son again. I walk to the car like someone heading for their execution.

The second day towards home the trailer brakes jam with my husband behind the wheel- I know, poetic huh? The tire explodes on the trailer on the downhill slope into Butte, MT.

Smoke flying, rubber shedding…he is not hurt, but boy is he going to make me pay for prophesying that the trailer was unsafe. He buys himself dinner, but not me. I have a bag of peanuts and a glass of OJ from the hotel bar.

That night, he gets 2 beds in our room, and is in his own all by himself. He has the TV on, and it is another CSI episode about someone burying their girlfriend alive. I go to sleep with my husband's voice explaining how, "He could have killed that woman, so much better." Ok, is it just me, or does CSI have a lot of crime scenes where the husband kills his wife?

The 4th day of the 2 day trip home, my husband asks me to check the tire pressure on his vehicle, while he pumps gasoline. I am checking the front driver's side tire, when I see him get inside and start the vehicle. I thought maybe he was starting the air conditioning while he finished pumping gas? But, he slips the car into gear and guns the vehicle forward, while I am under the car! My head makes contact with the fender, which luckily pushes me away from the moving vehicle and the tires! He turns the car into my body, but I was already rolling away and he misses me. I screamed, "What in the hell are you doing! You almost ran me over!" He yells back at me, "I was moving the fucking car!"

I didn't tell you, I took the names and phone numbers of the people working in the restaurant, before I got back in the car with him. I didn't tell you either- that I wrote down the name of the gas station where he tried to run me over. I emailed it to Ann, and my friends who were watching out for me, from the various hotels we were staying at. I asked Ann to take this information over to the county sheriff's office. Officially, I was working for the city, driving their new PD cars home. Maybe they would take the domestic violence more seriously if I got hurt while on their payroll…or, my son could file a wrongful death suit- from a doggone long ways away if I never made it home.

A week later and $4000 over budget, we arrive home. I discover he has another interview out of state, has bags packed, and there is paperwork that looks like he is trying to shift his financial burdens onto my small shoulders, and leave.

I also discover a love note hidden inside his police vehicle- and it sure isn't to me.

Welcome to my Nightmare

He comes home late, like almost 8pm, I am alone with him in the house, and he says he needs to "talk" with me. The kitchen table is between us, and he has his service weapon in his hands, loading the clip, racking the gun, then taking the clip out, over and over. He tells me in that cold and reptilian voice I have come to know so well, "I know you are a smart girl and you'll get exactly what I am talking about." Click. Rack the gun. Click. "I am going to get another job, out of this fucking place." Click. Rack the gun. Click.

"I need you to be a good girl, and think about my career, and my future." Click. Rack the gun. Point it across the table at your wife. "I will take care of you. I am moving on." "You're not stupid. You're not going to jeopardize my career. You know what is good for you." The gun is pointing at me. He asks me then, "Unusual? Don't you have anything to say back?" Face to face with The Monster, his gun, and a kitchen table that seems about only an inch wide, I respond very slowly and quietly, "No. I don't know what you are talking about. You just need to do what is good for you." He stands there staring at me, the gun casually aimed at my stomach across the top of the table. Then he walks out the front door with his service weapon still in his hands.

I don't know how long I just stood, holding onto the table, after he left.

Three days later, I file for divorce, and try to get a protection order from our superior court judge. He denies it. See, he has been shooting and having lunch with my husband before. I am downstairs in the courthouse, crying and afraid to leave. The court server is worried about me and calls the sheriffs dept.

Three deputies respond. When I relate how my husband has made plans aloud to me, about burying me alive and getting away with it- one of the deputies gets pale. He explains that he heard the same story, of how my husband would kill his wife, during the 4th of July festivities. My husband shared this story with the officers for like 45 minutes in detail. They thought he was full of shit. Oh my God!! Another of the deputies tells me- he was in the restaurant when my husband snapped on me. He saw the whole thing! Why in the hell isn't anyone doing anything!! No one will give my son and I a place to live, once they learn who my husband is.

Meanwhile, I was continuing to search everywhere for contacts, shelters, organizations- ANYONE- who would hear what was happening, see the corruption, and help us to escape. My son and I were hoping that with all the violations of the requirements to be a law enforcement executive, the city would fire him- or, as in most cases of small town police corruption, would offer him a "resignation". If P.O.S.T (Police Officers Standards and Training) or the state's Police Chief Organization would perform the 'policing' upon their own, I would not have to expose the domestic violence to be safe. He would be asked to resign and move, or in jail, and we could stay put. I also began writing the state's coalition against domestic violence, but discovered they are only an organization for promoting legislation. I would strongly suggest that you too, look on your state's web site, and review the present laws against domestic violence, abuse, and rape.

Ann tells us she will make room at her home for us. The local county deputies encourage me to file for the protection order over in the next county, and Ann offers to drive with me. I am denied again, and am given some document none of the officers have ever seen before, forcing me to appear in court with my husband to dispute the necessity for a protection order. Not just that, but I get home and discover that "someone" from the clerks office called ahead and warned my husband I was attempting to get a protection order.

72

I make an appointment the next morning with the city attorney, and re-advise him of everything. He asks me, if I have knowledge of any "illegal" activities that my husband is a part of? I tell him I was asked about missing weapons by the sheriff's dept. and the pawn tickets discovered in his police vehicle for weapons. He sold vehicles of his that he did not have clear title to finance his escape to another law enforcement department position, and committed fraud and misrepresented his credentials on his federal application. He did not disclose his restraining orders, protection orders, bankruptcy or foreclosures. He did not disclose he was reported for child abuse.

You see, all along we had been hoping, they would at least fire him for his fraud, and he would then leave town. I would never have had to step in front of his gun about the abuse.

I meet with the YWCA victim's advocate and learn of how archaic laws are about rape. Words like "knowing" between the victim and the rapist, and penal to vaginal penetration. Anal sex in this state is against the law, but not penal to vaginal penetration between people who "know" each other. Beating your wife with a stick the size of your baby finger was legal until just a few years ago! I realized that must be why he raped me like he did. By law, he found a way to rape his wife and not be charged. I went from her office to the state police post with my journal. The officer had a conflict of interest, it seems he met my husband during a crime scene investigation and my "account" is sent to another county for review.

Ann comes home livid, telling me my husband ordered her to "serve" me his papers for divorce, contradicting the directive they received from the city attorney to stay clear of any proceedings. She took it directly to the city attorney and told him of the violation. The city attorney still does nothing.

I am getting harassing emails from my husband through his police dept email account. He calls Ann into his office, and cusses her out about me not responding to his email. I copy all the emails, and again report to the county detective. He advises that without a protection order to support me, my husband can contact me any way he wants!

Ann's job is threatened by both the city attorney and by my husband, for helping my son and I. Ann tells my husband after his threats about her job, that if he shows up at her house, for any reason, she will shoot him first- and not need to question.

I discover that the same judge who refused my protection

order and called my husband to warn him, is the judge assigned to my divorce, and he did not recuse himself!

I find a bullet casing in Ann's driveway right next to my car door. Did you know that is one of the ways that corrupt law enforcement cops "mark" their targets? Again, I reported it to both the county and state police. Nothing was done.

My husband tells Ann, he was over speaking to the YWCA victim advocate, inquiring about me? We all felt he disclosed this info so I would know he was watching me.

I discover that my file has never even been given a case number, and that it was forwarded to the state's attorney general's office, only to be left on a desk there marked, "Conflict of Interest" again. I called the state's victim coordinator only to get a run around about conflict as it seems the AG met my husband at some chief convention. Right. Oh, and that my husband was to be a witness on a high profile murder case.

Lets add insult to injury, I would need to pick up the paperwork and find a county that was without conflict to review my own case! I stopped contacting the attorney general's office by phone, and put everything into emails that I could copy, and keep!

I advised them that it is not the responsibility of the victim to seek out jurisdiction for their case! The AG then sent the case right back to our home town.

The high profile murder case the attorney general's office referred to was placed on Ann's desk long ago, by my husband. Ann told me she believed he was hoping to sabotage her career by proving her incompetent, getting the murderer acquitted by her own inexperience and lack of investigative skills. My husband was taken off the list of witnesses long, long ago.

Ann, my son, and I watched as my husband's behavior really became erratic, self destructive, like career suicide. He began not showing up at the office, and parking the chief's vehicle in front of a woman's home and at her place of business. Good news travels fast, and juicy gossip is like FedEx overnight. Talk is all about him having sex on duty. People started going to the city attorney's office, complaining also to the mayor. No one would dare approach my husband with a rebuke.

I learned from a website- abuseofpower.org that the smaller the town, the easier it is for a corrupt law enforcement officer to abuse. Small towns are collectively afraid to do anything about an officer gone bad, and very often, pass him on with glowing reviews to the next unsuspecting town or city. After saving my emails from the Attorney General's office, I used the information I learned about the state laws

and statutes regarding domestic violence, rape, and assault- to bad-
ger their office until I learned that they indeed transferred my case to
another county far up north. I then began searching for a domestic violence program/shelter in that area. It took being relentless in searching
for me to find the help I received- and boy was it in the nick of time! I
found a fantastic legal advocate who had 19 years of experience, including in officer involved domestic violence. Then, I found a team with a
federal agent/law enforcement officer, giving seminars to government
agencies educating them about enforcement of domestic violence law. I
wrote to them about my case, gaining their contact info by pretending I
was an advocate who attended their last seminar.

When they received my letter, it was a red flag for them to inter-
vene- as my case greatly resembled another police chief's wife, who
was murdered by her husband- after months and months of requesting
assistance just like me.

A guilty verdict is received for the child murder case, and the
whole town breaths a sigh of thankfulness, except my husband.
I heard he stood in a corner of the courtroom, cold, sullen and
angry. Ann thought that he may be considering "suicide by cop".
That is when a bad officer has painted himself into a situation he
may be held accountable for- and chooses to fight or make a stand
against other officers, forcing them to shoot him. He knows if he
shows up at Ann's to hurt me, he will be shot. He is driving around
town late into the early hours of the morning, past her house, and
I think she is right about him choosing a guns blazing finale. Ann

may no longer have her career for helping us. We know he will go after her when we go, and we both cry. She tells me she would not have done it any different, but I worry for her protecting us, and what he will do to her later?

Before I ran my oldest son left me a message from college. He said, "Thank God he married you Mom. Anyone else, he would have killed. Only you could have gotten away!" Although we have plans and assistance to escape at the end of the week, we leave now, before he tries a desperate move.

I had been married 1 year and 5 months.

I learn that a law enforcement officer can gain access to phone records and GPS. Did you know that cars made after 2006 have a GPS built in? I disposed of my phone when I ran, and bought a throw-away one in the next state. Did you know that using a store reward card can be traced? Yep. I then began my long career of making up new names to gain access to store points, and fake addresses gotten from spotting rentals that were vacant, or homes in foreclosure in neighborhoods of stores I needed to access. Did you know that stereo stores may have the equipment to check your car, for hidden GPS devices- like old cell phones taped to your vehicle? My car was thoroughly gone over before the helping agency would pass me onto a secure location.

Exit Strategy

I leave in the early hours of the morning following the verdict, and take nothing but back roads and random highways, crossing back and forth through state boundaries. I miss the chance to phone in that I am leaving, as I have thrown away my original phone, so it can't be traced. I deliberately travel where there is no phone reception, as I am not sure if a GPS might be attached to my vehicle. I look for old highways where there are no cameras installed for traffic monitoring. I buy the first of many "throw-away" phones, and try out one of many aliases I will use to misdirect and mislead. There is this incredible hollowness about everything that touches my senses. Everything about me feels dull and numb. I try a drive thru fast food restaurant, but have to pull over and vomit alongside the road, all the while being afraid that if I stop long, he will catch up to me.

I arrived at my check point a day early, and when I call in discover that the federal agents within the area where I was living were on high alert! It seems they had my husband under observation, noting his increased erratic behavior, and thought when I could not be found, he had killed me. I am raw and cold when I am greeted by my new case manager. She seems like a marvel comic super woman, an Uma Thurman with zebra striped fingernails. It is so totally unreal I am laughing and crying at the same time! She shows me the text messages from various law enforcement agencies looking for me, who thought something terrible had happened to me.

Pinch me someone! I am not in "Stepford" anymore! The real world just showed up in stilettos and a huge hug! I feel like a paper doll-crumpled, thin, and pale. The first thing I notice is there music on the radio. Songs, bands- I haven't had any music inside of me for a long, long, time.

It makes me sad to think of how vacant I had become, and I cry several times before they finish with my car, and I head onto my next destination. I remember waving to the stars in the sky-thinking, I am alive and waving to all the friends I am leaving behind, to hide.

Did you know, within 6 months of a person being in hiding, they lose almost their entire support network of friends? Statistics show that victims who are in hiding more than 6 months return to a world void of their original friends? It seems that people cannot fathom the idea of anyone being in danger and away- and it becomes an additional burden for the survivors- to create a new support network.

I meet my next contact, Angel, and she suggests we take a small hike in the forest. I am thinking, "oh my God. When is the last time I was able to take a walk, go somewhere, and not be looking over my shoulder?"

We get ready for me to proceed to the shelter where I am to be an intake, and I have a panic attack, leaving the woods. I freeze in my car, and cannot move. My chest feels like I have an elephant on it, and I cannot breath!

My hands are numb, I can't feel my arms, and I think I am going to die…or my chest is going to explode! I vomit out the window. I am soaked with sweat, and shaking violently. This is the beginning of my body reacting to the fear and stress I have been subject to for over a year.

I move into a shelter. I learn that an agency is monitoring the movements of my husband, and, I am told he will not get another executive position in the state I am moved to. That's a huge relief! Thank God! They still have not formally reviewed my case, and there is no case number for it. I am grateful at least, that we are alive and out of his way.

My laptop is swept and looked at for spyware, and it is discovered that "someone" was using the tools within my laptop for webcam, to spy on me unknown. I learn that present made laptops have GPS ware built in, and I had my laptop erased, the GPS removed, and tape put over my web lens. I only just now turned it on, almost 3 years later, to write this book. It still gives me the creeps, that someone was watching me.

Noise seems to amp up my PTSD, and I start to look for active ways to stop my body from reacting. I go out my first day and get a Java Chip Frappachino, as I promised Uma I would do something for myself. I take a walk in the park next to the shelter, and give a small thank you to God. 1st- a safe bedroom at Ann's. 2nd- a safe house in a safe state. I pray my new super women friend's can wreck justice.

Gimme' Shelter

No one can break you into shelter life. No one. Not all shelter's house just domestic violence victims and their families. With the latest budget cuts the bureaucrat's passed- many shelters also must take in homeless, mentally ill, addicts, and people released from incarceration, to make ends meet. One of my case managers- Teri, advised me wisely, "Don't think you will make friends within a shelter. Everyone here is in a crisis, and should be tending to their own business- the business of getting over and through their crisis. You will find people here who will hate your forward progress, and try to stop it. Stick to your own business, and you'll make it through." Teri is a wise woman. I broke this rule once- and the woman I thought was my friend tried to end my stay at the shelter, and tried to ruin my outside contacts. It hurt, but Teri was so right!

I did escape with my dog, and a local kennel offered to house her close to the shelter. The first time I picked her up, we sat in the front seat together and huddled like we were prison camp refugees. I brought a peanut butter sandwich and slept in my car that afternoon with my dog. I would leave the shelter, pick her up, and sit in the car together with her for hours. I had no money, no where to go, knew no one. We just sat together until the day ended, and my curfew said I needed to be back to the shelter.

Some communities have safe pet programs, places working in cooperation with local shelters and kennels to house victim's pets for safekeeping. This program was confidential, and separate from the local county animal control. I volunteered at the kennel who kept my dog, and although I cannot name them here- THANK YOU SO MUCH!!!!

I agreed beforehand- that I would not email, text, or contact any family or friends- for fear they would be easily watched by my husband and his minions.

Gosh- it is so quiet and so lonely, to lose all your friends, family, because of violence. I am lucky that both Uma and Angel did text me and keep in contact. It is very lonely to move, not see anything happen to the perpetrator, and watch your life fade away.

My paperwork is forwarded to another county for review. I have some hope that someone will move forward to press charges against my abuser. I am told that there are a lot of high powered officials in the shadows, looking into my case. Then, I also hear back that the judge who told my husband about the protection order will not close our divorce, and ordered me to appear instead, or will order a warrant for me.

It is devastating news, and I now fear I will go to jail because I won't go to the state/town, and be an easy target for my husband. It is a roller coaster of "that's good. No, That's bad."

Uma asks me, how in the world I got away? She said she had not ever seen so many things stacked against someone, and then seen so many "God things" before, like with my case. Angel said I have awesome karma! I don't believe in karma, but I do believe in Jesus! You know, I believe the coaching confidence I got, was from my faith. Every step, every letter, note, journal entry, I prayed about. I guess the only full time confidante I had throughout it all, was God.

I have had a hard last two days. The concussion syndrome from my head injury has me in bed, sick and vomiting. I celebrate my birthday in the shelter, and one of the young women case manager's gives me a book of cowgirl poetry, thank you. I miss my children, I miss my friends, I am invisible.

A Little Faith

I have a new church! It is huge- like 5000 in their congregation, and I can go forward for anonymous prayer, and never see the same prayer group twice.

You go invisible church girl!

Every time I go forward, I get an amazing uplift from the people who pray for me, and I begin to notice that things I see are a little less gray!

I think there is a time, after we face someone evil, that we try and try to understand the why of it? I cannot wrap my head around "Voldemort's" blatant sabotage of his career and everything he lied to create? Even before I ran he was destroying his career.

ANSWER: Because he believed he is so powerful, so untouchable, he is daring them all to do something! Just try it!

I receive a message through my case manager, that the lead investigator within the state police dropped my case, stating for the record that I didn't wish to press charges! Interesting, because this very detective told me a story which involved his ex-wife, and her near drowning incident in which he was negligent.

It is very hard to tell your abuse to someone who has issues close to the border as well. What a great effort from Uma, who retrieved all my case records from the stuff I forwarded to her before I ran! Thank you again!!

She forwarded all my case documentation to the state law enforcement board. Collusion is the new word I now have for my vocabulary.

Re-victimization is another new word for what happens to a victim required again and again to re-tell their story to bull shit investigators who are not really committed to the investigation. Can you sense a bit of bitterness and frustration? I knew you could!

I saw a text passed back and forth between the women who were advocating for me, and it was kind of inspiring. It said, "do you think we are witnessing charisma, with the way everything is happening for our girl?" Oh how I hope God is still listening!

One of the ladies from the shelter attends church with me, and we pray together for her concerns that she has shared with the prayer team. "Surrounded by so much wickedness, please help me have peace. God of remembrance, in this much darkness, make my little light go a long way."

I get a call from Angel as she found someone who needs yardwork, housecleaning, etc. will pay cash, and she'll give me a reference! I finally have an income, and am able to have a purpose! I begin cleaning and cutting wood, pruning trees, and have a little bit of money. I get invited to stay local, and possibilities for other jobs occur.

I make Jayne Dough business cards and begin dog walking. I think it is the first time since my marriage that I feel productive. There is no one speaking death over everything I put my hand to. They examine my case more closely now that I have escaped, and think it may be longer than 90 days for me to be in hiding. Problem is, the program I am in is only good for housing me 90 days.

I learn something scary today, my husband's brother is on a federal "watch list" for the activities he has been involved in during his career in law enforcement.

Thank God I did not go to him for help! Thank goodness when offered an avenue for escape which led to the area he is an officer, my gut said no. I also realized that there are a lot of people within the program I was relocated to, that are afraid of the circumstances of my case. I need to be very careful as to who handles my progress.

I find there are people who just want to be involved because it may become a case of notoriety, others that are frozen in fear and overwhelmed by my story, and rendered useless.

It is very lonely in the shelter. I learn it is common to find people who "shelter surf"- meaning they go from program to program as they do not wish to get on their own feet.

Others are very jealous of any forward momentum another has- and instead of cheering for another's small steps forward, they will attempt to sabotage you. I begin my lonely journey as the "invisible woman" and don't disclose anything about who I am and what I have been through.

A little tip I learned: have you ever noticed how many cameras there are within the business' in your city? Look up and check it out. There are cameras at intersections, banks, pharmacies, and along the highway. I read that security cameras are set at a certain height to use later in case of robberies, fraud and such. But ladies- they are set for 5'10 to 6' tall perpetrators. I would suggest if you have a VIP abuser who can gain access to such- start wearing hats that have a brim or bill that will obstruct an overhead camera view. Also- I am very small in stature, and slight. I began wearing layers that camouflaged my shape/appearance, and changed my haircut and color right after I ran.

Politics- a Dirty Word

I have had several trips to the emergency room by now. PTSD is a very real disorder, and I have it in spades. When women fight in the shelter and raise their voices I feel like an elephant is on my chest, its hard to breathe, and my blood pressure becomes so high it is close to a stroke. I am having real trouble sleeping after being raped and woke up by someone trying to hurt me. You cannot get medical treatment most places and not give identifiers. You cannot get prescriptions without identifiers either. For some of us; we really need the assistance that medications can give to help us find relief. I learn that my advocate's job is in question, and she is the only person I have outside communication with! It appears that when others within her DV program hear of my case, they are attempting to breach my confidentiality to gain access to my potentially "high profile" criminal case. In refusing to compromise my confidentiality, her job is now threatened. I will lose one of only two people who have not been afraid to assist me because of my husbands V.I.P. status! I get very sick from the stress and it turns into pneumonia. I feel lost and forgotten in the silence her director imposes, as Uma battles the politics my case has created. I remember praying to be reminded that God is faithful, and I have come this far with His help. I believe Lord, help me with my unbelief!

A protocol is developed that allows Uma to conduct my case and continue to keep my confidentiality from the rest of the staff. My case is only to be for the directors' eyes and Uma's. The program I am in doesn't have a budget for any counseling, and Uma arranges with her agency in another state- to provide me with telephonic counseling.

It is such a relief to be able to talk about the chaos and the anxiety of being in hiding and not having any identity.

I meet another woman in the shelter who confides in me that she has been running from OIDV (Officer Involved Domestic Violence) for twelve years! She has not seen her family for all this time. She had to give up everything and everyone she knew to be safe. After being moved from multiple states to avoid detection, she has no one from her original friends anymore. Twelve years when she discovers in the shelter that her abuser is dead, and she can go home!

I kept hearing the echo of how lonely it has been for her.

As they pack to go home her daughter cannot find the stuffed animal she came to the shelter with. We begin to look through each community room, and it is nowhere to be found. I get involved in the search and we finally find it, the girl and I; stuffed in the dollhouse in the children's play room. Her Mom is so overwhelmed to be going home, I offer to color with her daughter so she can complete her paperwork. As they get ready to go to the bus station, the young girl gives me a raven's feather she found in the yard for a present. I still have that feather as a bookmark in my journal.

Even though I am safe, I am still married to "Voldemort" and he has control of the judge presiding over my case. I hear through the FBI that my husband is refusing to provide discovery, and the judge is supporting him. I will have zero from the divorce, zero retirement, zero support, and the judge orders me to appear! I am not safe to appear within the county let alone at the courthouse. It is like I am being ordered to appear at my own execution, and I don't go. I have to let the corrupt judge and my husband win, and I default on my divorce.

I do start to advocate for myself in other ways. Together with my new counselor Amy, we brainstorm on how fund and grant money for medical attention and counseling expenses can still be monitored without revealing a confidential witnesses name and identifiers.

Several medical/mental health and wellness providers meet with Amy to discuss my idea, and it is approved. I become Jayne C. Dough, Pt # 00-000001. I can now receive medical care, hospitalization, and counseling, have a baby (not unless it's Immaculate Conception) and receive assistance for prescriptions. All which, can be tracked for monitoring grants without revealing me! Amy, you are awesome! She went to the meetings and negotiated for the change.

I hope every advocate and health care worker who reads this will consider assisting this change to happen within their health care communities. Please assist domestic violence victims with medical attention who need to remain nameless for their protection!

The shelter where I reside is having internal issues, and it is reflected in the community of residents. There is fighting and bickering, stealing of others belongings and the staff is not monitoring anyone.

I take the few things I have now and lock them in my car. I am threatened of bodily harm, and sleep in my car because I am afraid I will be harmed by one of the women while I sleep. I haven't slept in 3 days. It becomes so bad I drive myself to the emergency room but a panic attack freezes me in my own car, and I cannot move to open the door and get out. I call Amy from my car, but she can hardly understand me as I struggle to breath and not black out. She calls the hospital ER desk, and a kind someone comes out to help me. I spend the night in the hospital, and get my first sleep in 4 nights. The staff splitting is so acute that no one within the shelter even notices I am gone until I return the next morning. I am approaching the 90 day deadline and nothing had moved forward about my case. Where in the heck am I going to go?

I think it all feels like "you know what" hitting the fan, but I am too exhausted to duck.

Domino's Anyone?

There is major dissention within the staff at my shelter. The house manager's behavior is tyrannical, and the staff begins to sabotage her authority to the detriment of our services and case management. Most of the women are savvy shelter surfers who harbor and hide food, leaving nothing in the fridge at the end of the day. There are verbal and physical confrontations among the women clients, and I begin to lose weight as I struggle to find a way to access the food we are provided in the house. Since staff is busy combating each other, no one watches as women begin stealing from each other.

I catch a woman going through my meager belongings, trying to find out who I am to see if it is worth money. I lock myself in my car at night to sleep, as I am afraid to close my eyes in a room filled with 6 strangers. The house manager checks in a woman with HIV just to scare the young staff about contagion. The house manager tells me that Uma and Angel will not be contacting me anymore. I am cut off from the two advocates who have been so crucial for me to keep it together. During this chaos, many of us do not have any real case management, and others legal issues go unaddressed.

I am at my counselors when I receive a frantic message from "Donna", a housemate at the shelter. It seems that a staff member just dropped her off at the courthouse, where she needed to file a protection order against her spouse. The staff member went out to lunch, instead of accompanying her. Donna is sobbing and I can hardly understand her as she begs me to come to the courthouse, as her husband showed up and went after her! She said no one at the shelter or the hotline answered the phone, and she is afraid. I race over to find her outside the courthouse, hiding in the shrubbery, and although I am afraid of the police, I go with her to fill out a police report. The shelter never returns her frantic message. We are missing from shelter programming while in the sheriff's office, and the shelter never knows we are gone! I wrote down the entire incident of me rescuing another resident and no one from the shelter answered the batphone. I gave a copy to Amy because I know that all of Gotham City and the shelter staff are going to be really pissed they were caught screwing around, and my roommate was left at the hands of her abuser. Sure enough, Christmas Eve the director for the shelter has a private meeting with me. She says they are out of beds, and they are "outing" me immediately!

Funny, but there are 4 empty beds in the shelter, and two other women leaving today?

I discover an email within one of my disposable email addresses, warning me to run. My husband is moving to the state I am hiding in! It appears Voldemort deduced my whereabouts from "someone" in law enforcement disclosing who helped me escape. He tracked down their field office and was within 36 miles of knowing where I was hiding!

I provide a complete disclosure to the sheriff's department about Donna's circumstances and being left at the courthouse. This sheds additional dark light upon the shelter and the manager's performance. She begins to focus her poison at me. She shuts the heat off in my room, and begins targeting me for extra chores, and writes me up again and again. I am ordered to leave, but I refuse to exit, as there is not even a plan for where I am to go, and my abuser knows my whereabouts. Not too good a time to be sleeping in the park in my car either. Amy intervenes again and puts a stop to me leaving. A mechanic volunteers to take a peek at my car, discovering that someone had sabotaged my brakes, and it isn't safe to drive yet. I go to church on Christmas Eve just desperate to find some peace, and have a panic attack at the candlelight service. I can't get out of my seat to go back to the shelter. I am afraid to be alone in the house with the manager, and afraid also, that I will be sleeping in my car in the winter if she has her way. I can hardly remember what all happened next. My church and Amy scrambled to get my brakes repaired, and the shelter turned the heat off in my room so I wouldn't be comfortable. There was a major snow and ice storm that closed the international airport and all the highways leading out of town. Even with the west coasts perfect winter storm, the shelter manager exited me! Not a single road open, major county wide power outages, and road closures, into the storm. Some incredible Providence moved mountains in the nick of time: Amy searched and found a wonderful dealership that when hearing about my plight did all the repairs on my car for cost! My pastor and his family met with me after service, prayed for me, and gave me the promise they would cover the expense to repair my car so I could run. Amy put up the money for me to have a room in a motel, as it took me 2 days to make a 12 hour drive in the storm. Finally, the family who be-friended me, kept my dog, and helped me find my smile; they let me move into their home for the 10 days it took to fix my car and wait for the storm and the damage it caused to be cleared away. This family is so wonderful! We still keep in touch and I love them! It was the first family I felt in 4 months– thank you!!!!!

As I travel, the sidewalks and towns roll up, as the storm that wrecked the northwest follows me as I run again.

I will confess, in the middle of the re-victimization by the house manager-I thought several times about ending my life. I hadn't thought about it while I lived with the Monster, but I did while I lived under the supervision of another one.

My practice of journaling pays off. It is funny how we get placed in places and people's lives– and sometimes never know why. Angel and Uma contacted me when I left. It seems the shelter manager told them I didn't wish to speak with them anymore– that I didn't need them? Angel asked me to write a complete description of the incidents within the shelter where I was exited. I heard several months later that the board did a formal investigation, and all the people involved in what felt like very personal persecution to me– had been doing it before I ever became a case number. I was the only one who wrote it down. They have terminated the people who have been abusing their power and authority. It took a long time for me to feel anything about the news. I just felt too bruised from their abuse to feel vindicated.

A New Zip Code

I drive through the new community, new state, new zip code, and just have a small spark of hope, that this will not be like the last place I was housed. This new shelter has a guesthouse where my dog and I can live together. I cannot explain how it felt to have her up on the bed (even though it is against rules for pets to be on the furniture). I think it is the first time I really slept since I began to run. My dog has always been my protector. Now, she is a savior of sorts. I am assigned a case manager, and fill out all the paper-work for Uma and Angel to be back on board and helping me! This place has it's own thrift store where I can get clothes suitable for the winters here. Oh my word, I am finally warm enough! I receive a suggestion to attend a church in a neighboring town- and it is a little piece of heaven for me. I think it is this last little piece that helps my inside gyroscope to finally settle down a bit. I really feel like I am being helped, even though so many laws only assist domestic violence victims if there were charges pressed and their perpetrator was found guilty. I cannot access any of the assistance programs because they never ever charged my abuser. The FBI cannot officially help, same deal breaker. I continue to remain the invisible woman.

When someone is a victim of a high profile abuser, the process becomes much longer and very complicated. I learned that I may have to change my identity 2 to 3 times, to keep it muddled in the "grid" and harder to track. I may have to keep moving, as once his fraud is discovered, he moves, resigns, and relocates. It is also smart to keep moving, as a traveling target is harder to hit. I learn to never give my real birthday, place of birth, and I Google the next place I wish to go- to pick out the most popular name in the phonebook, to blend. I do not get a bank account, as they are easy for a high profile VIP abuser to follow. I keep track, whenever I am not in the shelter; of parked cars with people in them, license plates, people without partners around me, and where all the exits are in stores and businesses. I look for empty houses when I walk my dog, too. Empty houses are places to hide: for me, or someone looking for me. I also can use their addresses for discount cards at grocery stores with a fake name.

I begin searching for an attorney to get advice. I speak with an attorney with the Coalition Against Domestic Violence, and she's familiar with my case. She has spoken with the director of the ACLU, who said I have a case. When I pursue it I find they won't help me, they only do class action suits with lots of people. Well crap, most of the women who have had discriminatory law enforcement and did not receive due process are either dead or seriously underground. I write my specifics and appeal to several civil attorney's, but no one will take my case against the state. The corruption and lack of enforcement went all the way to the state attorney general's office.

I am having a difficult time making personal connections within this community I am relocated in. I know I am still afraid of being discovered by The Monster, and I struggle with letting that fear stain and taint every smiling face who greets me. I seem to do better meeting people in church, and so I begin little baby steps of trust. I accept lunch invitations in public places I am familiar with. I find myself sitting in my car with my dog a lot, and wondering what on earth will become of me? I think of a special lady in church who between herself and her husband, really threw me a lifeline I couldn't refuse. Vicki and her husband became my first friends, and not because I was invisible either.

Vicki reminded me that I had places and parts of me that were worth knowing, and I think I laughed again in their home.

Rattling of Gates and Bones

I cannot remember where I was or what I was doing when I noticed my cheapie cell phone had a voice message? Immediately I could feel the hair on my neck start to prickle and rise, and I remember I was afraid to push the button to listen. I think I was outside walking my dog, cause I seem to recall feeling the security of a tree holding me up as I began to lean up against it for support. The voice was Angel's. She was worried for me. Someone had phoned her private number, leaving a message for me? The message said they had my dog, somewhere way up north from where the other shelter used to be. They wanted to meet me, to give me my dog back. She wanted to know if I was alright? Am I safe? Please call her back. I know I ran back to the shelter but I cannot remember how I got there. My dog was in a domestic violence program with protections for confidentiality, and just to be double-safe, we registered my dog in Angel's name. Someone had gotten into that secure system, and accessed my dogs' information, and was following the trail through Angel. I had a panic attack in the shelter, my first one since I arrived. I can still see the shelter staff around me as the paramedics attached the EKG equipment to me. Oh my God please don't take me to a hospital, all the identifiers! Words like stroke, and heart attack, were whispered around me as I fought my own body to gain control. I remember gasping to the paramedic, if he knew "Waking the Tiger"? He did, and began the somatic process of helping me off of the ledge. Even now, my chest gets tight to tell you. The Monster was looking again.

"Waking the Tiger" and "In An Unspoken Voice" are books written by Peter A. Levine, Phd. I have been blessed to be guided to an incredible Somatic Experience Counselor- Melissa. Somatic counseling is based on the theory that, "trauma is neither a disease or a disorder, but rather an injury caused by fright, helplessness and loss that can be healed by engaging our innate capacity to self- regulate high states of arousal and intense emotions." Yes, my panic attacks are like a weapon of mass destruction. The paramedic assisted me by using humor, to distract the fright/flight initiation, and I was able to interrupt the launch sequence button "from the ledge". I learned in that room at that moment, I could reverse that sequence, I could interrupt my body's

104

extraordinary reflex, and I was going to make it! Thank you Meliss!

If I could be having coffee with you right now, and you were telling me how you just escaped from an abusive relationship, I would have to ask you- are you in counseling? I know I would not be here, now, writing this book, Living- if not for effective counseling. My life would be fighting dragons with plastic swords, without it. If you haven't gotten help, please do.

The Call Back From Darkness

I decide that I will not run again. Even with him looking, I won't give up the peace I have found here.

Little pieces of "Miss Who from Whoville" began inching out from the darkness.

I began reading aloud to children in the shelter, and playing games with them outside.

I rediscovered my love for reading, and although I could not use any real ID to check out books from the library- a rebel librarian on the "down low" loaned me books without any paper trail. I was reading three books a week, like I did in college. A dear, dear friend in the form of my most favorite book, finds me again- Stargirl, by Jerry Spinelli.

One of the children in the shelter was having a birthday. He asked me, if they were getting two kinds of ice cream, how about if he asked for my favorite? Nothing like strawberry birthday cake plus two kinds of ice cream to chose from, right? I did not know what kind of ice cream I liked. I could not even remember a taste that was special for me. It made me cry. I am like a soldier who comes home from war, and can't remember what his favorite dish is, for his loving family to make for him. I shared it with my case manager. We decided I needed to make a field trip to the local grocery store. My goal- to hit the freezer case to see if I could recall which ice cream was my favorite. I was kinda excited, looking at it that way. It wasn't like ice cream was stolen from me then. It was more like an adventure on the discover channel. I remember walking back and forth, trying to have a memory like kids "try" to go to sleep for Santa. You know what I did? I bought three- chocolate chip cookie dough, Reese's peanut butter cup, and double chocolate brownie. Me and the children had ice cream headache's, and I know which one is my favorite now!

Someone gave me flip flops. Now, that's not a big deal to you, I'm guessing, right? But, I remembered that I had not worn or owned any flip flops during my marriage, because you cannot run away from The Monster in flip flops. I realized I had been wearing running shoes since the first incident. You cannot run over a hay field and through the woods, in flip flops or high heels- He'll get you. So, February fourteenth, Valentine's Day, 6 month's running- I put on my first pair of flip flops. Oh, and I asked for nail polish to paint my toes.

Which leads me to another discovery. I was asked if I would give the presentation at our organization's summer fundraiser. A testimony about the abuse and my escape. I know so many people blessed to have lived without the first or second hand knowledge about domestic violence, are under the impression that it only happens to undereducated minorities. Perhaps my testimony would enlighten our program supporters, that violence is not a respecter of persons? I had heard that a woman from the state I originated from had lost her life when officials did nothing to intervene in her behalf. Her story was a lot like my own. I decided if I could convince one person to help, intervene, one person to "see" another invisible woman before it was too late, I was going to speak.

But, if they were getting me a dress for the gala, what was my favorite color? What size was I? I could not remember. Most of my clothing are things I picked up at the thrift store, way too big for me, so I looked larger in a profile, or a drive by. I had almost all black clothing- to be invisible. Volunteers from my shelter met me at the thrift store, where I tried on dresses in many colors, and discovered my right size.

I remember standing in front of a mirror, looking at myself in this little Porsche red dress, and crying. I forgot I could be pretty.

I forgot my favorite color is red. And when my case manager gave me socks in tie dye to make me smile…I changed my mind. My most favorite color, is tie dye!

I am blessed that this shelter has progressive programs, which will help myself and others get back on our feet. There is a program to educate and assist those who have been financially abused- and here is the first time I understand, that I have also been abused this way as well. We have weekly group counseling, and it is very different to meet others who are struggling, or who have overcome their abusive situation. You see, I am the only one who is still invisible. We still haven't found a way to safely change my identity.

"I once heard a tale of a man

Who split himself in two.

The one part never changed at all;

The other grew and grew.

The changeless part was always true,

The growing part was always new,

And I wondered when the tale was through,

Which part was me, and which was you"

Children of the Mind
Orson Scott Card

Voice of One

As soon as I decide to make the presentation, the words come chasing after me, until I ask for a notebook and make them stay on the paper. I have my dress, thank you Melissa. I am going to wear heels as I have no plan to run, but I am taking the tie dye socks to wear right after my presentation. Melissa is coming, in case I come apart- thank God! Vicki is coming for support as well. Teri and I go up into the mountains for the morning of- and I am surprised that this state looks a lot like home does to me. I felt like I have known for a long time that I will be asked to speak out about the violence I have seen. This will be the first time I have spoken of the abuse, to people who are prepared to listen. It feels pretty big, and I feel pretty small.

The master of ceremonies introduces me by a first name I was given a long time ago, in another shelter. He asks the photographers to respect my confidentiality, and to take no photo's of me.

It was so quiet, and my heart is hammering in my dress as I take the stage, and tell my story. I still don't remember my delivery, but I do remember the faces of the attendee's, donors, volunteers and journalists as my tale comes forward. I was told later I did an incredible presentation, but I didn't hear a word I said. I ran it out again in front of all those people. I re-lived it. Melissa was so terrific to take me outside immediately following my speech, to the creek. I took off my shoes right away, and went barefoot, shaking and trembling outside to breathe.

Amazing things happened then, beginning with going to the Ladies Room. A woman reached under the bathroom wall, and I thought she needed toilet paper? As I went to give her some, she took my hand instead. She whispered that she wasn't brave enough to leave her abuser. She was afraid to start over, and be without everything. She apologized to me, for not being brave. We held hands as I offered to pray for her, right there, with the bathroom walls like a catholic confessional. She was crying. I waited for her to leave the bathroom, before I went out myself. Vicki introduces me to Loretta, who has a large hunter/jumper facility in town. Loretta offers me the opportunity to ride horses again, and gave me a recommendation for my first job! Another person came up to me and hugged me later, whispering she was also a survivor, and thanked me for speaking out.

I danced in my tie dye socks, I looked people in the eye, I sang.

I have a voice, and I am ok. I know what Cinderella felt like- at the ball. I think I am not quite so invisible anymore. Well, at least tonight.

The GPS of Jayne

I have been an invisible woman for a little over two years, before a path was discovered to change my identity. I began writing this novel right after I left the last shelter. I can take long hikes, and bike rides, and leave my journal on a tabletop, not bury it anymore.

A wonderful person offered me the opportunity to move out of the shelter, and into his home. He is a church going man, who is kind and we became prayer support for each other. Even though I now have a place of my own to live, we still meet to share "God" stories and pray for our friends.

I have a wonderful job, with people who laugh, and they hired me before I officially had a name, thank you! Although I have come a long way, I still feel the need to keep my footprints light. He is still at large, and will never be charged. I don't have whiplash from looking backwards anymore, but I still check my proverbial rear view mirror, to make sure.

I am in counseling, and so appreciate that support. Sometimes I still have nightmares. Years later, I recall another fragmented and frightening moment- when he uses his forearm to choke me into unconsciousness during sex. I felt strangled as I recalled the incident, and realized that to hurt me in that way, he made sure he left no fingerprints on my throat.

I still can have blinding migraines, and my hearing disappears on that side; the one he battered. I don't like being out alone after dark and I wonder if some things will always be different for me after this? I will never, ever watch horror movies.

I continue to struggle from the financial devastation that is a real and lingering part of my marital Armageddon. It is frightening sometimes to think, that I am starting over in so many ways, and with so little in the way of material things.

I hope this book helps others to have an understanding of the dark devastation of domestic violence, and that in a small way-this could make a difference.

I have contact with my children now, and it's like Christmas every time I connect with them! A few really close friends didn't give up for me, and I can embrace them now, and thank them, for not forgetting about me. I am so grateful they didn't lose sight or hope for me!

Every step I take now I make with a purpose. I know I am on a much brighter path now.

"May you recognize in your life the Presence,

Power, and Light of your soul.

May you realize that you are never alone,

That your soul in its brightness and belonging

Connects you intimately with the rhythm of the

Universe.

May you have respect for your individuality and difference.

May you realize that the shape of your soul is

Unique,

That you have a special destiny here,

That behind the façade of your life

There is something beautiful and eternal happening.

May you learn to see yourself

With the same delight,

Pride and expectation

With which God sees you in every moment."

To Bless the Space Between us
John O' Donahue

Suggested Links and Reading

"*The Gift of Fear: Survival Signals that Protect Us from Violence*"
by Gavin de Becker

"*In an Unspoken Voice: How the Body releases Trauma and Restores Goodness*" by Peter Levine, Phd

"*Healing Developmental Trauma: How early Trauma Affects Self-Regulation, Self-Image, and the Capacity for Relationship*"
by Lawrence Heller, MD

"*People of the Lie: The Hope for Healing Human Evil*"
by M. Scott Peck, MD

"*Blessing the Space Between Us*" by John O'Donohue

"*The Four Agreements: A Practical Guide to Personal Freedom*"
by Miguel Angel Ruiz

"*Stargirl*" by Jerry Spinelli

OIDV.org

Abuseofpower.org

Behindthebluewall.com

ncadv.org Lists state by state coalitions against domestic violence

feminist.org RAINN- Rape, Abuse, Incest National Network
information

womensshelters.org

vday.org

thehotline.org

Sobering Statistics

The prevalence of domestic violence IS sobering:

- Nearly one in four women in the U.S. reports experiencing violence by a current or former spouse or boyfriend at some point in her life

- On average, three women are killed every day as a result of domestic violence. More than 40 percent of female murder victims are killed by their boyfriends or husbands.

- Data collected in 2005 found that women experience two million injuries from partner violence each year.

- Women ages 20 to 24 are at the greatest risk of experiencing nonfatal intimate partner violence. They also experience the highest rates of sexual assault.

- More than 80 percent of victims of domestic violence are women.

- 75 percent of the people who commit domestic violence are male.

- Women who have experienced domestic violence are much more likely to have a stroke, develop heart disease, develop asthma- and drink more heavily than women who have not experienced domestic violence.

"I am over the passivity of good men. Where the hell are you? You live with us, make love with us, father us, befriend us, brother us, get nurtured and mothered and eternally supported by us, so why aren't you standing with us?
Why aren't you driven to the point of madness and action by the rape and humiliation of us?"

~Eve Ensler~
Author of *"The Vagina Monologues"*
Founder of the "One Billion Rising" Movement
onebillionrising.org

Cycle of Violence: Power and Control Wheel

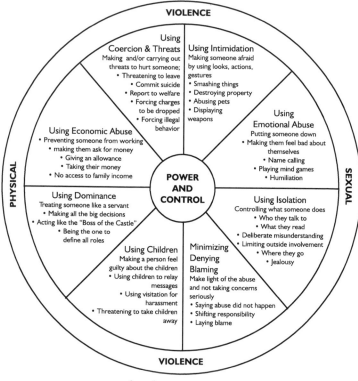

theadvocatesorg.org

Law Enforcement Power and Control Wheel

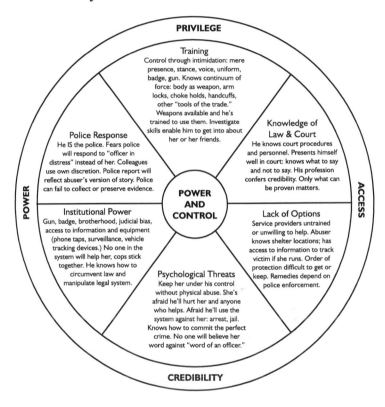

PRIVILEGE

Training
Control through intimidation: mere presence, stance, voice, uniform, badge, gun. Knows continuum of force: body as weapon, arm locks, choke holds, handcuffs, other "tools of the trade." Weapons available and he's trained to use them. Investigate skills enable him to get into about her or her friends.

Police Response
He IS the police. Fears police will respond to "officer in distress" instead of her. Colleagues use own discretion. Police report will reflect abuser's version of story. Police can fail to collect or preserve evidence.

Knowledge of Law & Court
He knows court procedures and personnel. Presents himself well in court: knows what to say and not to say. His profession confers credibility. Only what can be proven matters.

POWER AND CONTROL

Institutional Power
Gun, badge, brotherhood, judicial bias, access to information and equipment (phone taps, surveillance, vehicle tracking devices.) No one in the system will help her, cops stick together. He knows how to circumvent law and manipulate legal system.

Lack of Options
Service providers untrained or unwilling to help. Abuser knows shelter locations; has access to information to track victim if she runs. Order of protection difficult to get or keep. Remedies depend on police enforcement.

Psychological Threats
Keep her under his control without physical abuse. She's afraid he'll hurt her and anyone who helps. Afraid he'll use the system against her: arrest, jail. Knows how to commit the perfect crime. No one will believe her word against "word of an officer."

POWER

ACCESS

CREDIBILITY

www.abuseofpower.org

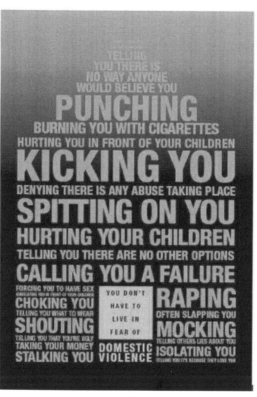

www.familylore.co.uk